Don't Miss Out On Any Avocado Milkshakes
The Art and Joy of Being a Film Editor

By Troy Takaki, ace
Illustrations by Annie Motel

For permissions contact: avocadomilkshakes@gmail.com

ISBN 978-1-365-41247-9

This book can be purchased at lulu.com

For Ronald Takaki

The greatest man ever

Special "I Love You"

to Warner West Takaki, Zoe Takaki and Mia Takaki

Special thanks to everyone that helped me with this little book:

Carol Takaki, Anastacia Goodin, Shannon Weiss, Dan Stoneberg, Amelia Allwarden,
Harry Yoon, Jun Kim, Judd Maslansky, Kristin Valentine, Kellie Cunningham,
Shanon Baker Davis, Thad Nurski, Yasmin Assemi, Shelby Hall and Felise Epstein

Table of Contents

Forward by Harry Yoon

I'm convinced that all great advice, at least the advice that you remember, comes in the form of a great story. When it comes to lessons learned in the cutting room, I can't think of a better storyteller than Troy Takaki. So many of his stories reflect his deep love and respect for the editing process. He's one of the only people I know that will interrupt a well deserved break between projects to edit something for free just because the subject or workflow on the project fascinates him. For Troy, editing is far from a job; it is a vocation. I think that is what makes him worth listening to. In every lesson he reminds us how transformative it can be to work those long, difficult hours not solely for money, fame, or status, but because we love what we do and want to be better at it.

Before We Get Started

The Tao of Troy

Why *The Tao of Troy*? I am not claiming to be a great philosopher, but I do live by a certain philosophy. Tao can be translated as "the way." Taoism can be thought of as a simple way to appreciate life and learn from life's experiences, living life like a river flowing downstream, taking the most natural path. If you do this, you will enjoy life and live serenely.

I know this all seems a little silly, but read my tips. Enjoy my stories. You might not only learn how to get ahead in editorial, but you might enjoy yourself while doing it.

Continue to learn

Before we get started, I need to tell you one important aspect of this book. It is really more of a companion book. In order to really understand how to make a resume, use an AVID, or cut two shots together please read:

Make the Cut: A Guide to Becoming a Successful Assistant Editor by Lori Coleman and Diana Friedberg   (a must read)

Jump-Cut: How to Jump-Start Your Career as a Film Editor by Lori Coleman and Diana Friedberg (another must read)

In the Blink of an Eye: A Perspective on Film Editing by Walter Murch

Avid Agility: Working Faster and More Intuitively with Avid Media Composer by Steven Cohen

Cutting it in Hollywood by Mitchell Danton, ace

Hitchcock by Francois Truffaut is an interesting read

There is also a film *The Cutting Edge: the Magic of Movie Editing* that you should watch.

A little history

I have been working as an editor for more than twenty-six years. Over that time I have worked my way up from Post Production Assistant (Post PA), to Assistant Editor (AE), to Editor. I have worked on television shows, features, documentaries, sizzle reels, wedding videos, music videos, you name it.

Around twelve years ago I started mentoring. I probably mentored people before that, but twelve years ago I started helping out with the American Cinema Editors (ACE) Internship Program for assistant editors that are at the beginning of their careers. Then two years ago, I started a mentoring program at ACE for editors and advanced assistant editors.

During these last dozen years I have given the same advice and told the same stories over and over. They have become more refined over time and are ever-evolving.

Recently, one of my mentees, Jun Kim, helped me out on a small side project - a sizzle reel for a director. Jun did an amazing job, and I was able to provide him with an enthusiastic recommendation to my friend, Harry Yoon, who had asked if I knew of any good assistants. When I found out that Harry had hired Jun, I emailed the two of them, "Little side projects are important. Do them. Give 110%."

Harry replied back, "Have you ever read *Harvey Penick's Little Red Book?* We should definitely create a *Troy Takaki's Little Red Book for Editing.* It could include all your great tips - each with an illustrative anecdote. Let's discuss."

The next day I started this book.

*Harvey Penick's Little Red book is a classic in golf instruction and advice.

Chapter 1: The Big Picture

Be early. Do great work. Be full of joy.

One time I met with an assistant editor who was having a little trouble finding and keeping jobs. We talked for an hour about all sorts of things, and this was the advice that I left her with, "Be early. Do great work. Be full of joy."

What does this mean?

There is so much in this business that you CAN'T control, but these are three things that you most definitely CAN.

When I say "be early," I mean all the time and with everything. If work starts at 9 am, be there at 8:50 am. If you are expected to have a continuity done on the last day of dailies, begin it on the first day of dailies. If you are asked to have stock footage by Friday, hunt it down on Tuesday. If you find yourself saying the words "I was late because of traffic," "I didn't have time to start the continuity because there were so many dailies" or "I haven't had time to look for the stock footage because I had too much sound work," then you are doing something wrong. This is a business that rewards results, not excuses. This is true both when you are the boss or the underling.

Here is what happened when I met with one AE.

I had agreed to meet an AE looking for advice on finding and keeping jobs. We agreed to meet for coffee at 9 am. I was there at 8:50 am. She arrived at 9:25 am. A lot of people would think it was okay if the times were reversed, i.e. if the AE that wanted advice arrived at 8:50 am and the editor showed up at 9:25 am.

I say that neither person should have been late.

Both of us should have walked in at 8:50 am. Or even better, when I walked in at 8:50 am, she could have handed me the hot Americano that she knew I was going to want because she had asked me the night before.   Be at least 10 minutes early for everything.

When I say "do great work" I mean do a top notch job, not just a competent job. If you are looking for stock footage, find the best stock footage. If you are making a continuity, make the best continuity. Think outside the box. Use all your resources. You might say, "But I always do the best job possible," to which I say, "Do you scrub and rinse the dishes before you put them in the dishwasher"? That is what you should be doing at work. Take a step above the normal. Lots of people can do "normal". Be better than that.

When I say, "be full of joy," I mean bring love and happiness to your workplace. Say "good morning" to everyone. Get to know everyone - the PA as well as the boss. Laugh as much as possible. Work with your door open when you can. It is easy for an office to become a negative, unhappy place.   Do everything you can to work against that.   This will not only make other people happier, it will make you happier.

If you start with these three concepts, everything else should fall into place.

Be humble

I worked my way up the ladder rather quickly. I went from not knowing a soul in the entertainment industry to Post PA, to AE, to Editor on a network show in two years. At some point my head grew too big.

I was working on an indie film with another editor, Rick Blue. Rick was a friend of mine. In fact, I had assisted him on a Movie of the Week (MOW) and he helped me get the job on that first network show. But this time we were editing for free on an indie film cutting 16mm. Rick had come up through video tape editing so he was new to film and because of this, I was much faster than him. While working with the director, I said something to that effect. I am sure that the way I said it appeared to be bragging and putting Rick down.

Later as we were walking to our cars, Rick started yelling at me, telling me I was just a kid. He had been an editor for ten years and I was just learning. Basically calling me a little shit. He was right. I was a little shit.

That night I decided to change my ways.

Now I try to be humble. I try to avoid putting down other people's work. You can do amazing work. You can even have a huge ego. That doesn't mean that you need to display that ego. It should never be a competition.

Be grateful

Always remember how lucky we are.   We get
paid to do something that we love.   Most people
don't get to do that.

Even during the longest, hardest days, we are still
making movies
(or television shows).

Be grateful.

Ask what you could do better

How can you get better at your job if you don't find out what you could do better? Most people are reluctant to criticize you unless you ask them for advice.

I was having coffee with Jun one morning.   I told him to make sure to ask the AEs what he could be doing better.   He replied, "I did that. Apparently I wear too much cologne." We laughed.   But that is a great example.
No one is going to tell you that you are wearing too much cologne unless you give them the opportunity to give you advice.

If you ask, they might tell you other things like, "I hate it when you are late." Or, "I wish you would learn Photoshop." Or, "You play on your computer too much."   You need to know these things. Open the door for people to tell you.

In fact, now you can start the conversation by telling Jun's story about, "too much cologne." It is kind of funny and would make the discussion easier.

Be Great

I always say that there are three types of people who work in post production. One third are "fine." They show up five minutes late and do their job. They actually work quite a bit. One third are "good." They show up on time. They pretty much work all the time. Then there are the third that are "great." They show up fifteen minutes early. They have their next show lined up. (Disclaimer: There is still the possibility that you are out of work. Schedules don't always line up neatly.)

Your first goal is to be "great".

Be around people that inspire you

One weekend my mentorship group went to see a demo of a new theatrical projection format.   The demo was really cool, but more important, we all went to dinner afterwards.   We chatted, drank, and had fun.

A colleague there, Dan Stoneberg, had recently taken a giant leap of faith in his career. He left a perfectly fine career as an editor on non-scripted cooking shows to be a Post PA on a feature. At face value, this was a big demotion - literally two steps down - in order to switch from one format to another. He was very excited about meeting other post-production people in different formats such as features, scripted television and non-scripted television. Their experience made him see his career in different ways.

Here is the analogy that we came up with.   If you stay in your format it is like being on a single train track.   You only associate with people on that train track. You might travel very far and maybe very fast on that track, but being with people that are on other tracks makes you see the world in a different way. You say, "Oh my God. Look at that track! And that one"!

Try and find a way to associate with people in other formats. This might be hard to do at first, but once you find one person, they will know others.

Chapter 2: Looking for Work

Don't be scared

Working in the entertainment industry is different than just about any other industry. The moment you start a job, there is a countdown to when the job is over. If you don't like this, maybe the entertainment industry is not for you. All of us go through times in our careers where we think to ourselves, "Oh my God. I am never going to find a job."

The good news is that there are lots of jobs out there, at least in LA. If you are good, you will find work.

Don't be scared to look for work. Everyone in the entertainment industry is doing it.

In June, I finished a film. My next film was starting in September. I could have had two months off during the Summer. Then I found out that the September film was cast-contingent. No cast, no film. I decided to find a summer job.

Here is the actual email I sent out:

Hey everyone,

I am finishing an awesome film for Universal, "Almost Christmas", on June 24 and I am available after that. I'm looking for something fun to edit this summer. Does anyone need some help? Have a pilot? Summer series? A film that needs a little help?

I might have a film starting in Sept, but it is not for sure.

And if I don't have a job, lets play golf or have drinks or something!!!

Cheers,
Troy Takaki, ace

Point being: don't sound desperate, but don't be afraid to send out an email. Personal emails are better than what I sent out, but it worked. I had a summer job ten minutes later.

Exploit the time off

If you end up having time off, take advantage of it.

Don't just sit around and do nothing. Even if you are doing fun things, work a little networking into every day. Go and see people for coffee or lunch.

Use the time to shadow other editors, or AEs.   Many of your friends will let you come and watch them work. They will love that you are interested in their process. In addition to learning something, you will get yourself out there. It is amazing the number of people who never take advantage of this.

However, it is important that you visit, have coffee and have lunch with people while you are working too. Don't just show up when you need work.   You need to have been going to lunch with your friends every six months to a year. It shouldn't be the first time you emailed them in five years. These are your friends, and they want to help you find work.

Chapter 3: Job Interviews

Head to job interviews extra super early

Like I said, you should always be early. This is particularly true when it comes to a job interview. The chances of your getting the job when you are late to an interview are very slim. It immediately shows the amount of care you will give the job if you are hired. Why would they hire someone who can't get to the interview on time?

For job interviews, I try and get within walking distance an hour early rather than just 10 minutes early. I get near to where the meeting will take place and then try to find a coffee shop. Then when it is 10 minutes before the appointment, I walk in.

However, you shouldn't actually arrive at the office more than 10 minutes early because they won't be ready for you. They might be in a meeting or you might have to sit in the waiting room next to someone who is interviewing before you. It could be awkward.

When I had an interview at 20th Century FOX for *Diary of a Wimpy Kid: Rodrick Rules,* I arrived at the studio one hour early. So there I was all parked and had time to kill at FOX. I wandered around, looked through the script, and relaxed.

Then when I arrived at the office, the Senior VP of Feature Post Production said, "Troy. You made it. We were worried. You came through the gate an hour ago." Little did I know, they receive an email when a guest comes through the gate!

I explained that I was sorry that I made them nervous, but that I always try to arrive an hour early to any job interview. Needless to say that was music to any post supervisor's ears.

But, I had learned this lesson the hard way.

It was a Saturday years ago. I had a job interview for a feature for Disney at 3 pm around 25 miles from my house in Venice. It should take 30 minutes to drive there on a Saturday. I gave myself an hour - 30 minutes plus 15 minutes "just in case" which should have gotten me there at least 15 minutes ahead of time.

I jumped on the freeway and there was an accident. The freeway was stopped. The next hour was torture. I was trying to get in touch with my agent on a Saturday. Sweating. Swearing.

I did arrive just in time, but I was a nervous wreck.

Never again. When it comes to the interview, never leave anything to chance.

Know the show, Story #1

In the early 90s, I was the post supervisor on the TV show *Tales From The Crypt*. It was a new season, and we needed to hire one new editor. Four editors were interviewing for the job. One of the four, Drake Silliman, was a friend of mine and called me. He wanted a few copies of the show to watch. This was a long

time ago, before you could stream any show. It was even before it was easy to rent one. Drake stopped by the office and I gave him a couple of episodes on VHS.

A few days later, we interviewed the four editors. He was the only one

that had seen the show. Needless to say his interview went much better than the others. He talked about what he liked about the show, a scene that he particularly enjoyed, etc.

He got the job.

Know the show, Story #2

From then on, I made sure to watch an episode of any show I was interviewing for. They will almost always give you a copy. Sometimes if there is only a pilot, they will make you watch it in their office.

So, when I got an interview for *Ally McBeal,* I asked for copies of a few episodes. They had me run by the office to pick them up. While I was there, I ran into the editor that was leaving the show. He was leaving to be an Associate Producer (AP) on another show so there was no bad blood. I had met this editor before, and we started talking. He told me what he was going to miss the most about editing *Ally McBeal* was the subtext. He explained to me how the text of the scene could be about one thing - a court case for example - and the subtext would be about another - such as Ally's relationship with her mother.

That night I watched the episodes and saw several examples of the use of subtext.

The next day I went in for the interview. The interview was going fine when they asked me about my thoughts on *Ally McBeal.* I responded, "I

love the use of subtext within a scene. It must be so much fun to edit".
We then talked about text vs. subtext for the next twenty minutes.

I got the job.   Later the producer told me I had gotten it because I had
noticed the use of subtext in the show.

Take advantage of any and all resources to get familiar with the show -
whether it's the show itself or the people who have worked on it.

Know the people

In addition to knowing the show before an interview, you want to find out as much as possible about the people working on the show. Find out who will be in the room during the interview. Look them up on IMDb, search for them on Deadline, Wikipedia, etc. Watch other films or television shows that they have worked on.

Whenever interviewing for a movie, I watch other movies that the director has previously directed. I often watch one of the more obscure titles.

Years ago, I was interviewing for a film called *The Brothers Solomon*. The director was Bob Odenkirk. Before the interview, I read the script and watched a few things he had done before, including an indie film titled *Melvin Goes to Dinner*. The interview was going fine for about half an hour. I felt it was coming to an end because he was asking the usual "Let's wrap this up" question: "Do you have any questions for me?" Instead of asking a question about the movie that I was interviewing for, I asked a question about *Melvin Goes to Dinner*. The next half an hour was a fun and interesting conversation about that movie.

They called during my drive home and offered me the job.

Scripts and props, Story #1

When you are interviewing for a movie as an editor, they will send you the script. I use this script both for research and a prop.

I was interviewing for *Jawbreaker*, one of the first features that I cut. I had read the script and put post-its on the pages where I had made notes, usually things that I liked. I brought the script with me and it was on the table in front of me.

One of the producers asked, "What are the post-its for?" I proceeded to open the script and talk about what I liked.   It made the interview go very well.

In addition to marking up the script and adding post-it notes on the front of the script, I write down topics I hope to touch on in the interview and questions that I have. If the interview has an awkward pause, I can just glance down at the script and start another topic.

It is good to have extra questions as they will often ask, "Do you have any questions for us?" Have a question ready, even if it is as simple as "How many days is the shoot"? A good question shows that you are engaged and interested.

Scripts and props, Story #2

I was interviewing for a film called *Stick It*. The director, Jessica Bendinger, was also the writer. In these cases, you really want to analyze the script and try and figure out what makes the director tick. I noticed that Jessica referenced specific songs and bands quite often in the script. Several of these were bands that I had grown up with in the Bay Area, including Green Day and Metallica. During high school and college I lived in Berkeley and played in punk rock bands. I had a lot of the same friends as Green Day and Metallica. We went to the same parties. I made sure to put post-its in places where these bands were referenced. I figured that would give me something interesting to talk about.

I arrived at the interview 20 minutes early. (This was before I adopted the one hour rule) I was a little nervous. I had just hired a new agent and this was the first interview that she had set up for me. They called me into the interview 10 minutes early. I was meeting with two producers and Jessica.

I really liked the script so I felt confident that I would have a good interview. However, I could tell that everyone was a bit on edge. Some job interviews feel like "business meetings" and others are casual like "meet and greets." This one started as the business type. Relatively early into the interview Jessica asked what I liked about the script. I flipped to one of my post-its which was one of the music references. I started talking about how much I liked Metallica and how I had played in punk rock bands. Suddenly the mood of the room changed. Jessica lit up. She became excited. Within 20 minutes, Jessica pulled me into her office and started playing music and showing me tone books.

One of the producers called my agent. This was only ten minutes after the interview was supposed to start. "Oh shit," my agent thought, "Troy didn't show up to the interview." But instead, the producer said, "Thank god you sent Troy. We had interviewed thirteen editors, but Jessica could not relate to any of them."

Scripts and props, Story #3

Back to the *Wimpy Kid* interview.

When I scheduled my interview for Wimpy Kid #2, they didn't have a script that they could release. So I bought the books. I read the first three books in the series, and I watched the first movie. In the end, they were able to give me a script, and I did my usual marking it up and writing questions. I also brought a couple of the books to the interview. These were purely props.

During the interview they asked me about the books. I told them about how before I was able to get the script, I read the books. I think this impressed the director and I got the job.

Love the show (or film)

No matter what, find something you love about the show or script before the interview.   This can never be a lie.   You need to find something that honestly makes you want to do the show and latch onto it.

Early in my career I interviewed for a movie with a script I didn't really like.   After the interview, my agent called the producers to see how it went, and they said, "It didn't seem like Troy really wanted to do the movie." They were right. I never found anything in the script that made me really desire to do it and that came through.

From then on when I am reading scripts, I look for things that I can fall in love with such as a character, a storyline, musical references, etc.   When I interview, I lean into that aspect.

If I don't love anything about the script, I don't take the interview.

Respect the show (or film)

Make sure that you respect the show you are interviewing for.

The other day, I talked to the director of my current film. I asked how the hiring of the crew was going. He replied that so many people had come into the interviews saying things like, "This is a family movie. It will be easy." He found that really condescending and rejected all of them.

Chapter 4: Being a great Post PA

Find out what snacks they like

Before the post-production office even opens, find out what the editor, assistant editor, director, really anyone that will be in the office, likes in craft service.

By far the best at this was my Post PA on *Diary of a Wimpy Kid: Rodrick Rules*. His name was Daniel Nussbaum. He was by far the best PA I have ever had. Even my other PAs would agree. Daniel moved from Post PA to 1st assistant editor on a huge tentpole movie in three years.

Before we started on *DWK,* he called my former assistants and found out what I liked to eat and drink: beef jerky and Tejava (unsweetened ice tea). He called the assistant to the director and found out what the director liked to eat and drink: PG Tips tea and frozen Mars Bars from England (the director was English).

When I walked into the office on the first day and looked in the fridge, there was a neat line of Tejavas. In the freezer there was a box of Mars Bars (imported). On the shelf there was a box of PG Tips and several packages of beef jerky.

We were all happy and ready to go to work.

Listen and think ahead

One day while working on DWK, the 1st AE and I were talking about what to burn into the screen on a phone in one shot (a phone or tv is often shot with a blank screen and you add what is to be on that screen later). Not wanting to get out of my chair I was yelling from my room across the bullpen to my assistant. Should it have the mother's name? Where would the incoming phone number go? My Post PA Daniel's desk was in the bullpen, so he could hear the conversation.

Ten minutes later I received an email from Daniel. It included an image of the exact kind of phone that was in our movie that he had found on the internet.   This showed what the phone looked like with text on its face.

Wow. I love that guy.

Make the office a nice place to be

Honestly almost nobody does this.   Daniel was really the only one that I can think of who really put effort into decorating the offices I worked in.

On DWK, he added all new lighting so that there was no harsh light.   He set up a nice table for lunch with a light that hung down like a dining table. He brought in plants.   In mid-December, he came in over the weekend and put up Christmas lights and hung snowflakes.

Get the lunch order right

This might be your most important job as a Post PA: getting lunch. Everyone has a method. Figure it out. Check all the orders before you leave the restaurant.

Here are three tips from my current Post PA:

- As orders come in from the staff, put them in an app like reminders so that you can keep track of who wanted what. It is also nice to have this information in the future so that you know what every likes if you have to order without their input.
- Bring a sharpie to the restaurant and label everyone's orders with their names before you leave the restaurant. That way you can be sure that you have every order and it is correct.
- Keep track of the staff's preferred beverages and put them out with their food. Also put out utensils. That way they can grab their food quickly if necessary.

Visit other PAs and see how they work

This is true whether you are a PA, AE or Editor. It is surprising how little contact you have with someone else in your position. Take advantage of the fact that you have friends in the industry. Even if you think you know what you are doing, why not learn how someone else does it?

Before we started on my current show, I had my Post PA visit Daniel Nussbaum in order to pick his brain. I figured he should learn from the best. Here is his adventure:

> *The first sentence out of Troy's mouth after hiring me for a Post PA Job was, "You need to meet with one of my former PA's, Daniel. He's the best." Troy immediately put the two of us in contact and we set up a time to meet up and grab some drinks. After doing a little research on Daniel, I was astounded by the impressive credits Daniel had under his belt in such a short period of time. After talking with him for ten minutes I firmly understood how he had gotten to that point.*
>
> *These are three things I learned from that evening that helped me become a better PA.*
>
> *-Learn what the people around you need before they even know that they need it. Your job is to make the Editor and Assistant Editors' lives less complicated so they can focus on their job. If you can anticipate something that they will need and have it waiting for them, they don't even have to think about needing it,*

freeing up their brains for what really matters: editing the movie or TV show.

-Create an environment people want to spend time in comfortably. *Nobody wants to work in a drab, lifeless office. It's even harder to be creative in one. Create a workspace that invites stimulating conversations, interaction and creativity.*

-Listen to what's going on in the office while staying out of the way. *If you are respectfully eavesdropping you might be able to chime in and really help out in a way that your editor isn't even aware of.*

Take the time to learn from other people. Shockingly few people do this. They learn on the job, but don't spend time shadowing and learning from other people.

Chapter 5: Moving from Post PA to AE

Help out the Assistant Editors

I must emphasize that you have to be a really good Post PA and be ahead on all of your work before you can use your extra time learning to be an assistant editor. If you are not a good Post PA, you will just look like you don't care about your current job. That does not help you at all.

My first Post PA job was on a show called *DEA*. It was a short lived show for FOX back in 1990. I didn't know anything about the business when I started and had to learn as I went along. I did my work quickly and early. I went to lunch with the editors whenever I could.

From the beginning I tried to help out the AEs. I would bring them their paperwork in the morning and ask if I could file it for them. I would put the lined script pages in. I would hole-punch the camera reports and put them in binders. I would put the call sheet on the wall. I know this all sounds mundane, but that is the point. To them it was mundane, but to me it was learning. It showed them that I could do AE work, and they appreciated the help.

Later they let me help input dailies, make outputs, etc. Because I had proved myself enough on the "mundane" tasks, they began entrusting me with more substantial ones.

I would stay late with them. Let's say I was done with my work and could leave at 7pm. I would stay and help them until they left. Back then the AEs would go to "Online sessions." These often ran from 6pm to 2am. I stayed late with them and watched the show slowly assemble in C-mode.* I didn't really do anything, but I was learning by osmosis. Some tape would be mislabeled. The AE would solve the problem. It is amazing how much I could learn just by being around them.

In addition to working as a Post PA on DEA, I would edit projects on the side. I would come in on the weekends and use the machines to cut wedding videos and music videos for friends. These are some of the best things to edit because you have to assist yourself. Often you have to problem solve: the videos were shot on different cameras, one was missing the sound, etc.

Once again you are not only learning the editing machine, learning to AE and learning to edit, but people see you doing it.

By the time *DEA* was canceled, I could at least fake being an AE. One of the people that I met on DEA recommended me for *Tales From The Crypt*, my first AE job.

* For all you newer people: If you don't know what "C-Mode" is, "C-Mode" was a way of doing an online back when we did them on tape. In "A-Mode", you would assemble a new "record tape" by putting the first shot from a "source tape" on the new tape then the second shot, then the third shot and so on. This would be fine if all the source material was on one tape, but if the first shot was on tape 001 and the second shot was on tape 002 and the third shot was back on tape 001 you would be changing tapes over and over and it would take forever. In "C-Mode", all the shots from one source tape would be put on the record tape and then all the shots from the next tape. So, all the shots on tape 001 would be dropped on the record tape checkerboarded, then all of shots on tape 002. In our example the record tape would have shot #1 and #3 dropped on it from tape 001. Then you would change tapes to tape 002, and shot #2 would be dropped on the record tape. This still took about five hours for a one-hour show.

Make your own luck

I used to think I was super lucky. How did I get that job on *Tales From The Crypt*? After *DEA* I was working in the "traffic" department at Lorimar. Lorimar had a department that arranged for drivers to move elements from facility to facility. I had paged one of my co-workers, Paul, to tell him something. At this time, he was driving by one of the facilities that we often dealt with, Laser Pacific. He pulled over in order to use their phone.

For any of you that don't know how a pager worked: before cell phones we all wore pagers. You could send someone your phone number and that person would find a phone and call you back.

While he was there, he ran into an associate producer, Robert Parigi. Robert asked him if he knew of any non-union AEs and Paul said, "Yes, I am just about to call one." Paul dialed my number and then handed Robert the phone. I got that job. My first real AE job!

Damn that was lucky. If I hadn't paged Paul at that exact time, he would have never run into Robert. For years I would tell this story as an example of how lucky I was.

But let's take a step back.   I put the effort into learning how to be an AE on *DEA*.   I spent time getting to know the coordinators in the "traffic" department. I didn't just call them with orders. I stopped by and became friends with them.   When my Post PA job ended, they asked me to join their department. I said that I would but only until I could find an AE job because that was what I really wanted to do.

Was it all luck? Or did I make my own luck? I have dozens of stories of being at the right place at the right time.   You will never be at that right place if you are not proactive.

Chapter 6: Being a great AE

Finish your assignments as early as possible

I was on the television show *Devious Maids* and the producer liked to have index cards on the wall with a short description of the scenes and he wanted these hung up when he came in for producer's cut.

About half way through the editor's cut, I would start asking my AE to make the cards. He would always wait until the last minute to make them. The producer would be walking in and he would still be putting them up. It would drive me crazy. Every day I would look at the empty board and think, "Why doesn't he just make them now?" I know some of you are thinking, "Troy is a bit OCD." The fact is this: If an assignment is due Friday and you can do it on Tuesday, then do it Tuesday. It takes just as much time.

This same assistant did the same thing with music and stock footage. I would give him an assignment, such as find stock footage of a restaurant. I would walk by him while he was doing nothing or checking his email, which might not be doing nothing but was annoying when I knew he could be looking for stock footage. Then the cut would be due and he would show me three restaurants. Whether I liked them or not, I didn't have enough time to find other options, which I found frustrating.

That said, when I asked this same assistant to cut a scene, it would be done two hours later. He was not slow. He just had his priorities messed up.

In fact, he listened to me about the rules for editing *Devious Maids* and did a fantastic job. He was a natural editor. A year later, I fought for him to be bumped up to editor, and he became one of the editors for season four.

It might look like he was rewarded for not being such a great AE, but I see both fault and potential in people. I am thrilled that he is editing full time now. If people call asking about him as an editor, I can give a wholehearted endorsement.

If you are not the first team on, follow the leader

This is a rule for television.   When you are the third team on, or are coming on during the fourth season, find out how they have been doing things in the past and follow their lead.

Find a continuity that the other AEs have been using. Even if you think your template is better, use the one that everyone is used to. Find out how they name VFX and use their system. Find out how they mark ADR and use their system. And on and on.

Sure, if their system is problematic, try to change it, but that should not be your first approach.

I had an AE that was constantly making everyone do things his way.   He was sure his way was the right way, constantly arguing with venders and the other AE.   Eventually, I stopped working with him because it was so frustrating.

Chapter 7: Moving from AE to Editor

Edit

After doing your work and being the best AE in the world, do some editing.   I mean edit anything: sizzle reels, wedding videos, your daughter's trip to the beach, a short your friend wrote and directed, the gag reel for the show you are on, the re-caps, or a scene your editor has already cut.

You might say that you are working such long hours that you don't have time. I don't believe you. Make time.

Not only will you become a better assistant and better editor, but people will start thinking of you as an editor.

When I was an AE, I cut my friend's unfinished student movie on the side. The editors on *Tales from the Crypt* noticed and started letting me cut scenes. Then when one of them left to direct another show, I took over and finished that episode.

But once again, be a fantastic AE!   It does you no good to be an average AE because you "really want to edit."

Watch your editor edit

You can also learn a lot about editing by osmosis.

When we cut on film, the first AE was usually in the room with the editor helping with the film trims. He or she was part of the editing process. The Assistant Editor was able to see the Editor's process firsthand.

Then came machines like the Montage Picture Processor. Usually on television shows there was only one machine per editor. The machine was huge and took up two rooms. Often that meant that the AE didn't have a room. Luckily for me, on *Tales from the Crypt* that was the case.

I had to sit quietly in the back of the room while the editors edited. There was nowhere else for me to go. And it was a three-two (three editors with two assistant editors), so I sat behind three different editors (five different editors over the three seasons). Without asking any questions, I studied their methods and styles.

I remember the first time I saw Lou Angelo steal a silent reaction from the end of a take after the director had yelled "cut". I was amazed. You could do that?

In fact, I loved the way Lou did a first cut. I mimicked his method of assembling a scene. I still edit my first cuts with Lou's methodology. He watched through all the dailies. Then he started again from the beginning of each take pulling a piece of film if he wanted it. He assembled it in a sequence, not worrying about the splices. There were often several readings of each line. Lou would then watch the sequence. It would be rough, but you could get the gist of the scene.

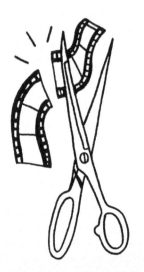

Next he would choose the line readings that he preferred and eliminated the others. Then he would watch it again. It wasn't until this point that he would do any trims. This way he didn't spend a lot of time trying to get a cut right, only to throw it out. Like I said, this is still how I edit the first cut of a scene.

On *Tales from the Crypt* I was also able to watch how the editors worked with the directors and producers. This was invaluable. The politics of a room are at least as important as the way you edit two shots together.

But along came AVID and shared media. Suddenly the AE had her own machine and was never in the room with the editor. The door to the editing room shut and you could no longer watch the editor edit. Everyone was saying, "This is great. Now the AE gets to try different versions on the side." Yes, but how is an AE going to learn all the tricks? How will she observe the politics of negotiating notes?

Now, not every editor wants someone sitting behind her while she does a first cut. But try to find editors that don't mind. Remember: don't ask questions. Be as quiet as possible. This is not about them teaching you how to edit. This is about you watching and learning.

And for all those editors out there: consider doing your AEs a favor. Invite them into the room every once in awhile. It is our job to teach the next generation.

AEs, if your editor invites you into the room, take them up on the offer.

Chapter 8: Being a Great Editor

Love to learn, Story #1

When given the opportunity to learn something new, I take it. Not that long ago, I received a call from my agent, "Are you interested in helping edit a documentary with Pauly Shore? It pays $3000 flat. Not per week. Total."

He had a cut of his movie *Pauly Shore Stands Alone* already but needed someone to finish it. He pitched it as only a few weeks worth of work. I had cut very few documentaries and loved the idea of getting better at it. I was not working at the time, so off I went to meet Pauly Shore at The Comedy Store.

He greeted me in the parking lot and led me through the kitchen and up some stairs, past pictures of great comics that had performed there and into a non air conditioned office. He showed me a trailer he had made for the movie. It was really good. Then he sat me in front of a sketchy FCP system and I watched some of the film. The editor that had cut it was very talented. It had potential. There was a movie in there. It just needed more story, more heart.

"What the hell," I thought, "a few weeks. I know the movie will be good. How can it hurt?"

Two months later, we had a cut. I learned so much about storytelling. We shot more footage than we needed. We added ADR lines to stitch the storylines together. We made things connect that were filmed days apart. Everyone should cut a documentary some time. Turning a mound of footage into a story is really cool. I learned so much while editing this movie. I use the lessons I learned about storytelling in my scripted shows.

I continued to help Pauly Shore off and on for the next six months - sound, music, DVD extras. *Pauly Shore Stands Alone* turned out to be really good. It was bought by Showtime and aired later that year.

I was nominated for an ACE Eddie for it: Best Editing: Documentary - Television.

Love to learn, Story #2

Another example of taking the opportunity to learn to edit something outside my normal medium is the time I was hired to edit a multi-cam show. You don't get a lot of opportunities to work on a completely different type of show.

It was November and I knew I had a show starting in January. I was planning to take a few months off. Then I received a phone call from a friend, "Troy, are you available to help out editing one episode of *Sam & Cat?*" *Sam & Cat* was a multi-cam show for Nickelodeon. I actually knew the show because my daughters watched it.

I said, "Hell yes, I'm available!" I had never cut a multi-cam show before. Would they really let me do it?

The funny thing is that I had been editing for about 23 years at this point. But I was still a little intimidated at first. During the interview, the live feed from the stage was rolling. Yes, in the producer's offices, they could watch a live multicam feed of what was being filmed.

The whole thing seemed very foreign but exciting.

They ended up hiring me, and over the next two months, I cut two episodes of *Sam & Cat*. It was so different from what I had done in the past. One of the most important things that I became good at was watching three cameras at the same time. That is how they watch dailies. You learn to shift your focus and decide which camera is important.

A year later I was editing *Agent Carter.* The show was a "single camera" show, but they almost always shot with three cameras and didn't cut between takes. Because of this, we usually received seven to eight hours of dailies each day. The other editors were overwhelmed. Not me. I watched all the dailies with the three cameras running multi-cam quad split. It was just like watching a multi-cam show. I could watch all the dailies in 2 hours and 45 minutes. That left me plenty of time to edit.

Now I watch all my dailies in multi-cam KEM rolls (a sequence where shots are cut into sequential order by setup, then take).

The point is: take jobs that are outside your comfort zone. They can teach you things that will help you when you are working in your usual medium or format.

Love working hard and long

This is especially true early in your career.

When you get your first breaks, it is often on crazy, understaffed, non-union shows. Love this time in your career and appreciate it. Hopefully, later in your career you will not be asked the impossible for such little money.

My second job as an editor was on the TV show *Walker, Texas Ranger.*

They were shooting in Dallas, but the editing rooms were in Los Angeles. The showrunner was expecting to spend the majority of his time in LA. Well, the shoot for the show proved to be more hands-on than he had expected.   He was in Dallas for the first four months.   In order to lock shows, he needed an editor there.

They shipped an editing system, and an assistant and I flew to Dallas. Over the next four months, I not only cut every other episode, I locked every episode.   There were times when I worked 20 hour days, slept for four hours on the stunt crash pads that they stored outside my office, and then worked another 20 hours. Over the year I ended up editing 17  of 24 episodes of the show from scratch and locking 21 of 24 episodes.

Every show had either a fight or a car chase in act 2 and act 4. Think of how much practice I got cutting fight scenes? What a unique opportunity! I became really good at editing fights and car chases.

Throughout the years, I worked on other television shows and features that had action sequences. I was never intimidated.

So, love and appreciate the times when you get pushed.

Chapter 9: Working with Directors (Features)

Directors are all different

I know this should be a no brainer, but you have to be able to adapt yourself to the director.

The last two directors that I worked with could not have been more different and they were both great directors.

One came from theater and was very free form. Any of his ideas could take on a life of its own and could send us off on a tangent if we were not careful. I also had to watch out for outside influences. He invited lots of people into the cutting room to give notes and offer opinions. Some of these people wanted to make an impression by having a "great idea". It was very important for me to control the cutting room and keep us on track.

The other director came from animation. Everything was very planned out; very controlled. My job was to turn his thoughts into actions.

Luckily both of them let me be a huge part of the process. The point is to learn and then adapt to what is best for that director and for the movie.

The director is not always right

I know we are all taught that the director is god, but she is not. The film is god.

I just ran into a post supervisor that I know. We started talking about a film she had just worked on. She complained about the editor. Apparently the editor constantly fought for every whim that the director had. That wasted time and money.

Sometimes as an editor it is your job to talk the director out of things.

Now, of course there are directors that you can never say "no" to. But even they want someone to stop their crazy ideas. That director will also appreciate that you want to protect the film.

Directors are long term relationships

You need to think of directors in particular as people you want in your lives for a long time. They will hire you over and over. So it's important to nurture this relationship, even when you're not on a movie together. Have coffee, drinks or lunch with them every once in a while between jobs.

Just as important, they will often want you to read scripts. Take that assignment seriously. Sometimes they just want your opinion. Sometimes they want notes. But read the person and the situation. Do they really want notes or do they want a cheerleader? Both are perfectly fine.

It is not unusual for a director to ask you to cut a sizzle reel (also called a "rip reel") for a project they are pitching .   These are short trailers cut from other movies to show what the movie might be like.   It is basically an evolution of a "look book". A look book is something directors bring to a meeting that shows the tone of each character and the overall movie. It is often made from clip art.

The important part is that it is something you do for directors when they ask, often for free. You want to do it, and with a smile on your face. You love these directors.

And remember when they get jobs, you get a job.

Chapter 10: Working with Producers (Television)

Get to know them

When I refer to television producers, I am talking about showrunners or the producers that give notes in editing. They are the bosses of editorial. Just as in features, the director is the boss. Most television producers are great, but not all of them.

I have worked with several television producers that were not very nice. Usually, I never worked with them again. But I am going to tell you about one that I swore that I would never work with again -- and then I did, and now we are friends.

I had worked on a television show with this producer years ago. He would often snap at you and tell you that the edit you made was stupid. I just put up with it and bit my tongue. I tried to avoid him at all costs. And I swore I would never work with him again. I got a feature during the hiatus and did not return to his show.

Seven years later, I got a call from an AP asking if I was available for a pilot with this same producer. I guess it was kind of like childbirth, I forgot how painful it was. Also, I wanted to work with the director of the pilot. So, I said, "Yes".

Well, the director and producer ended up not getting along. On the first day of the producer's cut, we had made it through about one act of the producer yelling out notes before the director stood up and said, "I can't take this," and left. Everyone took a breath. Then we started again. After about the tenth note that this producer phrased in a condescending manner, the other producer said, "You better be nice to Troy or he might quit, too." I turned and said, "Oh he can't hurt me. What is he going to do, fire me"? You see I was doing this between two features. I kind of had the upper hand. That didn't make the producer act much nicer, but it made it so that I could laugh at the whole situation.

I ended up spending a lot of time with just the producer while editing the pilot. I found out that when other people were not around, he was calmer and nicer. We talked about musical theater and other subjects that were important to him. I realized that I needed to make him consider me as an equal for him to respect me.

I found this often works. Be strong but nice. Talk to producers about things other than the show you are working on.

Chapter 11: The Difference Between being a TV Editor and a Feature Editor

Get to know the television show that you are editing

Every television show has rules and a style. This is very important. When you watch an episode of *Law and Order,* you feel comfortable with it. If you had turned on *Law and Order* and it was edited like *Glee,* it would seem just plain weird.

So when you are editing a television show, it is important for you as the editor to learn that style. This is very different from editing a feature or a pilot, when you are allowed to define the editing style for that project.

When I worked with Marc Cherry on *Desperate Housewives,* I learned this lesson. Marc has steadfast rules: dialogue should be on camera, never cut away during a joke, even if the joke is three sentences long, never pre-lap, there had better be a very good reason to go to a silent reaction, the reaction had better be telling you something, etc.

At first the rules seem very restrictive, but I got used to them. Soon I understood that this style of editing worked very well with Marc's writing.

Years later, I cut a pilot for Marc called *Devious Maids.* I used his rules, and I added another. The show was a prime time soap opera about Latina maids. We scored it with tango music as our guide. I cut the dialogue with a rhythm that was very *tango-esque.* From then on, that was the rhythm of the show. Subsequent editors had to follow the pattern.

You may ask, "But what about how I like to edit? I love pre-laps." Too bad. Learn to edit within the rules of that show. It will rarely result in bad editing. It will, however, introduce you to other ways of editing and make you a better editor.

A few years ago I was hired to do a few episodes of *Rizzoli & Isles*. Before I started, I watched several episodes. I studied how they used music, their editing rhythm, their editing patterns and the character traits. You would be surprised how a lot of television editors try to bring their editing rules and styles to a show rather than the reverse. Executive producers love when you give them a cut that looks and feels like the other episodes in that series.

Being a member of a team vs Being the leader of a team

When you are working on a television show, you are a member of a team. It is really important to remember that. You are one of two or three editors. The AP is your boss. Know the scope of your job and do it well.

When you are the editor on a feature, you are the head of post-production. You are the head of sound. You are the head of music. Being a good leader and manager are skills onto themselves. If you are not a great manager, that is a problem in features.

This skill is not the same on every movie. On some movies, the director works with the composer, and you see very little of the process.

On the last movie I was on, it was very important for me to be at every "show and tell". This is where the composer shows cues to the director that are works-in-progress. When this director went to see the composer by himself, the two of them would get pulled onto a tangent. One of them would say, "You know, like church music," and the next thing you knew several scenes would be scored with church organ. I realized that I needed to be there to keep things on track. So, I started to attend all the show and tells. From that point on we stayed on track. The score to the film turned out to be fantastic.

There are times in features when you are directing ADR, you are approving VFX, and you are directing inserts and second unit. There are times that you are instructing the music supervisor, music editor, and sound editor. Embrace the challenge and get good at it.

Some good editors are not great managers. It is important to be both.

Chapter 12: Tips on Editing

Point of View

While working on *Walker, Texas Ranger,* I not only became good at cutting fights and car chases, I also learned a very important lesson about point of view from none other than Chuck Norris.

There were two main characters in *Walker, Texas Ranger* : Walker, played by Chuck Norris, and his sidekick, Trivette. Chuck was very good at fighting, and while he wasn't bad at saying lines, he didn't give you a lot to work with when it came to silent reactions. In between lines Chuck only gave you a stoic look. Because of this, when I cut scenes with him in them I usually used other people's silent reactions, which were more expressive. I frequently used Trivette's
reactions.

One day my phone rang. It was Chuck. "Troy." Chuck said, "You need to cut in more close-ups of Walker." Chuck continued, "Remember the name of the show is Walker, Texas Ranger. Not Trivette, Texas Ranger." When we hung up the phone, I thought, "That was weird. What an ego."

I wanted to comply, but I still had to figure out how to make his stone-faced reactions work. My solution was to cut to Trivette first and then have him turn to Walker. I learned that if someone said something worrying and I cut to Trivette and he looked toward Walker, it made Walker look worried.

It wasn't until later that I really understood what Chuck was saying. *Walker, Texas Ranger* had to be from Walker's point of view. In every scene that Walker was in, you needed to see it through Walker's eyes.

This is not true in all scenes, or on all shows, or on all films. Most of the time the story or scene is told from a neutral point of view. The real take away is to always consider point of view when making decisions on how to cut a scene.

The Campfire Story

Editing a scene is like telling a story by a campfire.

When you are telling a story at a campfire, you minimize the text and describe all of the actions and subtext. This is the essence of storytelling. I believe that every scene is a short story. You need to be able to tell that story and not worry about the text. This might be easier for me to explain by example.

Recently, I took over editing an episode of a television show from another editor that had left the show. In this episode there is a scene when a husband comes home and finds his wife talking to their minister.

The text version goes like this: The husband enters. He finds his wife talking to their minister. He greets them and sits down. The minister has a few short lines about how his brother was also in the military and then the three of them pray. This is how the first editor edited the scene. Basically, all the minister's dialogue was on camera. There were very few shots of the husband or wife.

The campfire version goes like this: The husband enters. He hears his wife talking to their minister. He gathers himself and enters the room. He greets them and sits down. The minister starts to talk. Through looks between the husband and wife, the husband was saying to the wife, "What the hell is this about?". The wife gets mad and puts her head down with a look of, "He isn't even going to give this a chance." This all happens with the minister talking off camera. Through silent reactions you can tell that the husband doesn't want to be there.   By the time they start praying, he is looking out the window not paying attention.

What is the story of the scene?   The wife wants to help their marriage. She invites the minister over to talk to her husband. The husband is annoyed.   Don't worry about the text.   Worry about the story.

Watch all the dailies

These days they print all the dailies. The term "print" is from when they would actually print the film. Back then, printing a take was expensive so they would only print selected (circled) takes. These days, it is quicker and less expensive to sync and colortime all the dailies and send them to editorial.

Most editors have their assistants break out the circled takes and put them into a bin. These are the ones that they will use to edit with. I have even heard of editors that only work with the final two circled takes. Not me. I have my assistants put all the takes, circled and not circled, into the scene bin. Then I have them assemble a dailies viewing sequence with all the takes in the order that they were shot.

Before I watch this sequence, I read the scene in the script paying attention to the direction more than the dialogue. I know that when I watch this dailies sequence I am going to see the dialogue many times. I need to know if there is subtext that is not spoken.

Then I watch all the dailies for that scene including all the footage before the slate and after "cut". I study the development of the direction. I listen for off-screen direction and adjustments such as: "laugh when you say the line", "pick up the paper and then look up", etc. I need to get into the head of the director and actors. I have to be a detective.

While I am watching the dailies, I am cutting the scene in my head. There are great books that explain the rules of editing. Read them and adopt the ones that work for you. I am not going to tell you these rules. I believe in some of them but not others. For me they are starting points and nothing more.

What I mean by "cutting it in my head" is that I am figuring out the story of the scene and how to best tell that story. I am rarely concerned with when to use a master or close up.   I think about point of view. I think about line readings and how they are different from take to take. Sometimes I will even tell myself the story of the scene out loud.

After that I am usually able to cut the scene really quickly. All that time watching every take reduces the amount of time it takes me to assemble the scene.

Beware of the Notes - in Feature Films

In features you get notes from various sources: producers, the director, the studio, the director's friends, the director's nanny, etc. I have found that sometimes movies become worse during this part of the process. Of course this can also happen in television, but usually the notes in television come through one person or a small set of people. Because of this, you are not dealing with sets of notes put together by various groups of people.

You are definitely not going to try to make every random person with a note happy. Here is what sometimes happens in features. One person thinks that a joke's not funny and should be edited out, and four people think it is funny and should stay in. For some reason the one person that wants it out wins the argument. The other four people think, "It's just one note. Let's not fight about it," or, "I don't want to be labeled as difficult." I know this doesn't make any sense. But over and over the editor and director give in on "one little note". Someone doesn't like the freeze frames. Another one doesn't like this line or that line. Someone doesn't like a piece of music: "it's too Rock", "it's too on-the-nose", "I don't like brass instruments, so no horns" (a real note).

The thing about these notes is they often remove the more interesting, original, broad, cool elements. These are the ones which generally stick out. So, slowly but surely, the movie becomes duller and more generic.

You and the director need to remember this and fight against it. The purpose of movies is to make a film that is interesting and original.

How do you do this? First, pay attention to what the notes do to the movie. Are you taking out things that make the movie original? Second, make sure to point out to the director how the notes are affecting the film. It happens so slowly and in such small steps, neither of you might notice that all the small notes have added up to a huge disaster.

Remember What the Heart of the Film Is - Features

Sometimes I am brought in to work on a film that was in the process of being edited. Maybe the cut was not working at all. Maybe it worked okay, but the studio, producers or director felt it could be better. There are times when I come in, and the film was not edited very well, and I have to fix every edit, but often the film was edited well, but is missing its heart. This often happens because the earlier cuts of the film were too long, so they had edited out the parts that were not important to the plot. Unfortunately, these were often the same parts that were important to character.

First example:

I came onto an action adventure/romantic comedy. I was watching the cut they sent me and said out loud, "Wow, do these people (the romantic couple) even like each other? And if they do, why?" But the fight scenes with the bad guys were awesome!

I did a pass just focusing on the romance. I didn't touch the fights. I found little moments where the guy and girl got to know each other. Cute stuff. Then I found a "love theme" that   I
built into the temp score. I used another score that had several different

versions of that theme. I snuck it in at first, then let it build and develop into a full version for the kiss at the end.

I also did little things like move the bad guys' scenes later in the film, so that the audience could get to know the main characters without the distraction of the bad guys. But the most important part was really highlighting the romance.

Second example:

I was hired to recut a mother/daughter romantic comedy. By the time I came on board, the mother had been trimmed down a lot; especially the mother's interaction with the daughter's boyfriend. In some ways this was the least important relationship in the movie. The daughter/boyfriend relationship was the main plot. However, I realized that the mother's relationship with the boyfriend strengthened the daughter/boyfriend plot. The previous editor had trimmed down mother/boyfriend interaction so drastically that the movie did not work. The boyfriend was the plot, but the mother was the heart.

Let me explain my process when I come in to help re-edit a movie. I watch the current cut trying to have the least amount of background about the movie. I don't read the script or talk too much with the director. That way I only see what is on the screen. If I had read the script or talked with the director, I might have filled in the blanks while I was watching it.

Only after watching the movie with "fresh eyes," do I read the script to find out what didn't end up on the screen. I don't mean just the lines and scenes that might have been cut out, I mean intent, plot, and subtext. Then I have the director or producer tell me what they think the movie is about and what they want it to be.

At this point I start editing the current version. I try to add whatever elements are missing: romance, plot, tone, etc.

Once I have done a first pass, I watch the original editor's cut. I often find lots of lines and scenes that were cut out that could have really helped the film. Sometimes these need to be re-edited in order make them work. Sometimes the scenes were edited better by the original editor but were messed up during the notes process.

One important part of this process is to remember that as an editor brought in to do a re-cut, my job is not to change every cut to make it my own. My job is to make the film better, not to take ownership and show off. My job is to find the heart of the film and bring it out.

Chapter 13: Agents

When hiring an agent, meet with more than one.

When you decide to hire an agent, book three meetings before you go to the first one.   The reason for this is that if the first agent is impressive you might want to sign with that agent before you leave her office.   The only thing that will stop you from hiring her on the spot is that you have other meetings already arranged.

When I was changing agents a dozen years ago, I set up three meetings. The first one was with a small agency. They were great. I loved them and some of my favorite editors and best friends were with them. The next agency was one of the big ones. They represented lots of huge editors.   I met in a room with three agents and two assistants.   It reminded me of *Entourage*. Then I had a meeting with the third agency.   Here I met with the owner of the agency and two "below the line" agents.   I really felt comfortable there.   This is the agency that I picked, and I am very happy.   Who knows if I would have ever gotten to that third agency if I hadn't booked all three meetings before I started.

Later I gave the names of three agents to a friend of mine that was looking for an agent. He met with the first one and hired her. I asked why he hadn't met with the others. He said that he hadn't booked them and liked her. But now he didn't have any point of reference. Maybe she is the right agent for him, but maybe he would have liked another agent even more.

In a business where you will be changing jobs every few months, maybe a year at the most, your relationship with your agent will probably be the longest relationship that you have. I have been with my agent for 12 years now. Choose wisely, and gain wisdom through comparison.

The Agent/Client Relationship is Important

So many editors that I know don't put any effort into their relationship with their agent. I send my agent and her assistant Christmas presents. I call her while I am working, not just when I am looking for work. I try to go to lunch with her once a year.

It is important for your agent to like and respect you, and you will help this relationship by liking and respecting your agent, too.

Chapter 14: Co-workers

We are all on the same team

I have only had to fire one AE ever. He was mean to the Post PA. He treated her like a personal servant and yelled at her.   Now to be clear, a Post PA works for everyone in post. It was *how* he treated her, not what he asked her to do. He had her run personal errands. Once again, that's not necessarily a crime. I ask my PA, and sometimes my AE, to run an errand. This AE, however, would tell her to run personal errands and then yell at her if she took too long.

We could not fire him just because he was mean to the PA. There are legal reasons in addition to moral reasons. However, one night we were having a "friends and family screening." After the screening, everyone went to dinner. At one end of the table a discussion started offering suggestions about how to improve the film. One of the director's friends, a post supervisor, was giving suggestions that could have involved a lot of work for the assistant editors. My AE said to the post supervisor, "You better shut your mouth, or I'll punch you in the nose." Needless to say, once the director heard about this, he asked us to fire the AE. We were happy to oblige.

Take Time to Get to Know the People in your Office

This seems like a no brainer, but how many offices have you been in where you didn't really spend time to get to know the Post PA or the AEs and editors on the other teams?

I make sure to sit down and talk to every co-worker one at a time early in the show. I find out where they live. Do they have pets? Do they have hobbies?

Granted, some people I connect to more than others. But it is fun to be able to come into the office on Monday morning and say, "Good Morning! How was your weekend? Did you go surfing? How is your dog? Did you see that movie you wanted to see Friday?" This includes the director's assistant, the music editor, etc. anyone in the office with you.

While I was working on *Fool's Gold* in Australia, we took this to an extreme. Not only would we eat lunch together, we went on adventures: boat rides through the rainforests, hot air balloon rides. We rented cabins in the woods and visited a local water hole, a literal hole filled with water in a stream not a dive bar. (Although we visited lots of those, too.) We had a motto, "Don't miss out on an avocado milkshake."

You see apparently in the Philippines, they serve avocado milkshakes, which are a local treat. My second AE's friend had been in the Philippines for months. Everyone was saying, "You have to try the avocado milkshake." Finally on the last day, she did. Oh My GOD! It was the best thing she had ever tried. But she only had one day left in the country to enjoy them. So sad!

In Australia we didn't want to miss out on any avocado milkshakes. We exploited every opportunity, did it all and we did it early. It was so much fun. Talk about team building! We were all very close by the time we left Australia. We loved each other. Because of this, I think we all did better work and we sure enjoyed working on that film.

Have lunch together

Try to have lunch together. Too many of us eat lunch at our AVIDs.
Does it really save that much time?

There is one thing that makes having
lunch together much easier. Set up a
good lunch table at the beginning of
the show. On a lot of shows you don't
have control over this. I always ask
for an extra room just for a lunch table.
Getting everyone together for lunch
really helps with friendships and
morale.

Give People Compliments and Say Thank You

A lot of people around you do great work. Let them know.

One of my assistants, Joe Rockom, did an amazing job with temp music and sound effects.   I not only made sure he knew that, I made sure the other people in the office knew that too. He deserved it and it made him feel good. It also motivated him to want to put lots of effort into continuing to do great work.

I made sure that Daniel knew how great of a Post PA he was.

If you are on a television show, watch the other editors' episodes. Tell them what you liked about their episodes and their editing. It will not only make you know the show better, it makes you better friends with the other editors. A win-win.

Open your door and laugh

Ok, this one might not be for everyone.

Once, I came onto a show. They had moved the schedule around and needed an editor for just one show.

I stopped by to say "hi" before my official start date (something I will often do) and noticed that the office was very quiet. Everyone worked with their doors shut.

Because I was a spare editor, I was put into a small room in an area where all the assistant editors' rooms were. I didn't mind. I work where they put me.

My assistant Saleem was across the hall. If we opened our doors and sat at our AVIDs, we could see each other. Because of this, we started talking across the hall. We both have huge laughs so the laughter would float across the whole office.

Soon all three of the other AEs started leaving their doors open. They wanted in on the fun. Our corner of the office became full of joy and laughter.

Protect your co-workers

Unfortunately, sometimes things go wrong. Truthfully, there are often little mistakes every day.   There will be times in your career when you will work with people that have a desire to place blame or at least try and find out who's fault it is. At times, this can become a toxic situation. Personally, I try to avoid these jobs. Unfortunately, you often don't know this at first, but when you do end up on a job like this, try and get everyone to act like a team.

Whether you are the Post PA or the editor, use the pronoun "we" as much a possible.

"We are working on the continuity."

"We are getting a timing for the show."

And when there is a mistake on the timing sheet say, "Sorry, we made a mistake on the timing sheet. It will never happen again."

Hopefully, you can include the director and producers on the team, and they will start using "we" too.

Working in a toxic room

Unfortunately, there will be a time when you find yourself working in a toxic room. The concepts that I just talked about will not work or be appropriate.

Remember that at least you have control over yourself and your own attitude. Don't get sucked into the madness. There are times when your various bosses split the cutting room into different factions. If there are different factions, try and stay friendly with all sides.

I just had lunch with my former intern. She was working at a television show where they literally told her not to laugh too loud and not talk too loud at lunch. She was instructed to keep her door closed. The Executive Producer instilled a culture of fear. She finally quit. A week later she was still suffering from anxiety.

This is the worst part of the job. All I can say is survive it and don't go back.

Keep in Touch with People

After you finish a job, make sure to continue having a relationship with the people you have worked with. It is so easy to think that you are going to stay friends and then not do it. But it is also easy to stay friends. It just might take a little effort.

I have always had an annual lunch with Robert Parigi from *Tales from the Crypt*, an AP that I worked with as an AE over twenty years ago. I ended up editing a feature he directed.

Phil Neel was the AP on *SeaQuest* back in 1995. I see him at least once a year and make it to his Christmas party. We have ended up crossing paths every five or ten years. He put me up for *Ally McBeal* in 2000. I put him up for *Devious Maids* in 2013. Years later I worked with him on *Six*.

I play golf with Craig Bench (an editor I worked with on Ally McBeal), have breakfast with Andy Tennant (a director I worked with many times), lunch with David Bowers (another director I worked with many times); the list goes on.

It is also important to keep in contact with the people that worked for you too. Angela Catanzaro was my AE on *Hitch*. I invite her to lunch every few years.

This is only a short list.   The important thing is that I am not keeping up with these people because I want jobs from them. I keep up with them because I like to have lunch with them. It is fun.

Wine nights

I also keep in contact with a lot of people through what we call "wine nights". It started a few years ago when I wanted to keep in contact with some of the ACE interns after they were done with the program. The email list has grown to about 30 people.

We get together every six months or so at a wine bar next to a movie theater. It is a great place that is usually rather quiet so that you can hear each other.

At these "wine nights" we renew friendships and share stories.

During one of our first few wine nights, a post supervisor called and asked if I knew any Post PAs for a film. I looked over at one of our former interns, Rebekah Fridman. I actually took a picture of her and texted him. "I have a great one here!" In the end she got the job, and they even bumped her up to apprentice.

Start meeting with work friends every few months somewhere. Have fun!

Conclusion

Be early, do great work, be full of joy

I know I am repeating myself, but I am hoping that you now understand my advice.

Be early.

Do great work.

Be full of joy.

Troy Takaki is a film editor who has cut such box office hits as SWEET HOME ALABAMA, starring Reese Witherspoon, and HITCH, starring Will Smith and Kevin James, both with the director Andy Tennant.

Takaki moved to Los Angeles in 1990 to pursue his filmmaking career after graduating with a degree in cinema from San Francisco State University. He started in television, working on such hit series as "Desperate Housewives," "Ally McBeal," "Tales from the Crypt," and "SeaQuest DSV".

Takaki segued from television to feature films with such notable indies as JAWBREAKER starring Rose McGowan and Judy Greer, and THIS GIRL'S LIFE starring Rosario Dawson. His success in the independents led to studio features including DIARY OF A WIMPY KID: RODRICK RULES and DIARY OF A WIMPY KID: DOG DAYS for 20th Century Fox and the director David Bowers, NEW IN TOWN starring Renee Zellweger for Gold Circle Films/Lionsgate, and FOOL'S GOLD for Warner Bros. starring Kate Hudson and Matthew McConaughey, also with Tennant.

Over the years he has collaborated with many successful directors including Michael Apted, Mark Waters, David E. Talbert, David Semel and Charles Shyer.

In 2000, he was invited to join the honorary society American Cinema Editors. In 2016, he was invited to join the prestigious Academy of Motion Picture Arts and Sciences.

Annie Motel is the Vampire Princess of Hollywood. She works on The Blvd of Stars tattooing in a little shop and drinks blood only on Wednesdays. The rest of the days she loves to eat Lucky Charms, cheeseburgers and strawberry milkshakes. Annie lives with her cat Elvis and Vampire Prince Chris in a little pink bungalow behind a giant cemetery in Los Angeles.

Everyday, you can see Annie flying down the street in one of her classic Cadillacs. If you look closely, you can often spot her true love, the Ghost of Elvis Presley in the passenger seat beside her. She likes to listen to the cheesiest music while she cruises including Enrique Iglesias, Britney Spears, Marilyn Manson, Drake, Daddy Yankee, and Jason Aldean.

Annie graduated in 2009 with a BFA from the University of Washington with a minor in Acting. She lived and worked in Rome, Italy, Seattle, Washington, and New York City before settling down in LA.

She is a fine artist and has shown her paintings at La Luz De Jesus, Meltdown Comics, and The Gabba Gallery among many others.

Annie is a Coffin Girl of Coffin Girls, which is a modeling agency for creepy girls where 10% of the proceeds of the company go to charity. In addition, she has written a novel, "Wet Dolphin," and a collection of short stories, "Diary of A Hollywood Vampire Princess." They can be found on www.lulu.com by searching Annie Motel.

Annie only wears black.